# REMBRANDT

**LIONELLO PUPPI**

**GROSSET & DUNLAP**
**Publishers - New York**

First American edition published by Grosset & Dunlap, Inc.
All rights reserved
Translated from the Italian by Pearl Sanders
Translation copyright © 1969 by Thames and Hudson, London
Copyright © 1969 by Sadea Editore, Firenze
Library of Congress Catalog Card Number: 69-13388

Printed and bound in Italy

# Life

Rembrandt Harmenszoon van Rijn was born in Leyden on 15 July 1606, the last but one in a family of at least nine children. His father, Harmen Gerritszoon van Rijn, was a prosperous miller (he owned a few small houses, as well as a windmill near the Rhine – hence the name van Rijn), and his mother, Neeltge Willemsdochter van Zuitbroeck, was the daughter of a well-to-do baker. Perhaps Rembrandt showed unusual gifts as a child, for his parents seem to have wanted him to have a career outside the family traditions of trade (the eldest son, Adriaen, was to take over the family business). They sent him to the Latin School at the age of seven, and, on 20 May 1620, enrolled him as a student in the Faculty of Letters at Leyden University, which, although only recently founded, already enjoyed considerable prestige. However, Rembrandt soon abandoned his literary studies, and in 1621, with his parents' blessing, he began an apprenticeship with the Leyden painter Jacob van Swanenburgh, a mediocre artist, but one, at least, who could teach him the rudiments of his profession. In 1624, after three years with Swanenburgh, his artistic education began in earnest: he moved to Amsterdam, to work for six months in the studio of Pieter Lastman, a great admirer of Caravaggio and probably the most influential Dutch painter of the time.

In about 1625, at the age of nineteen, Rembrandt returned to Leyden, and set up his own studio, together with a fellow-artist, Jan Lievens, who was one year his junior. The two young men soon attracted favourable attention. Already in 1628, Aernout van Buchell, a jurist from Utrecht who was visiting Leyden, noted the high regard in which Rembrandt was held. Far more important, in 1630, Constantijn Huygens, Secretary to the Stadtholder, Prince Frederick Henry of Orange, visited the studio, and recorded his admiration. He had rarely seen, he wrote, ' a constancy and ardour for work equal to that shown by these young men, who do not even allow themselves the most innocent amusements of their age.' After commenting again on their extreme youth, 'still beardless and, in fact, by the look of their faces and physiques closer to childhood than to youth,' he remarks that Rembrandt – with whom he later formed a close friendship – was the driving force behind their joint venture: 'Rembrandt has the advantage over his colleague in the intelligence and liveliness of his impressions. His skill is such that, even in the limited dimensions he favours, he achieves a power of concentration whose equal is not to be found in even the largest compositions of his fellow-artists.' In these circumstances, it is hardly surprising that the studio was not only acquiring a considerable reputation, but attracting new assistants and pupils, such as Gérard Dou, who later became one of the most successful artists of the age.

On 27 April 1630 Rembrandt's father died. He now began to think of settling in Amsterdam, where he was more likely to be given important commissions, and where he already had promising connexions as far as patronage was concerned. His name still appeared in the archives as a resident of Leyden in June 1631, but there is evidence that by July 1632 he was living in Amsterdam, at the house of an art dealer called Hendrick van Uylenburgh, whom he appears to have known, both as a friend and as a business associate, for some time. The move to Amsterdam probably took place towards the end of 1631, since Rembrandt's first important commission in his new home – *The Anatomy lesson of Professor Tulp*, painted for the Amsterdam Guild of Surgeons – was placed in the Guild's headquarters on 31 January 1632. It was at Uylenburgh's house that he met Saskia van Uylenburgh, the dealer's young cousin. Both her parents were dead, and her father, a former Burgomaster of Leeuwarden, had left her a considerable fortune. A great affection sprang up between Rembrandt and the girl, and on 5 June 1633 they became engaged; the occasion is celebrated in a drawing. They were married the following year, on 22 June.

This was a period not only of great personal happiness for Rembrandt, but of professional success: his paintings were selling for very high prices, and he soon became extremely wealthy. He began to attend sales of works of art, where he made purchases of the most varied nature. We know from a work (1686) written by the Italian author Filippo Baldinucci that Rembrandt 'often visited public auctions, where he would acquire old-fashioned and cast-off clothing which struck him as bizarre or picturesque; and although these garments were sometimes full of dirt, he would hang them on the walls of his studio, among the beautiful and delicate objects which he also took pleasure in possessing.' We know from the inventory made of his possessions in July 1656 that his studio contained the most disparate objects, ranging from pure *bric-à-brac* to rare works of art: valuable paintings, drawings and engravings were to be found alongside Japanese fans, Venetian glass, statues and casts, stuffed animals, stones, shells and musical instruments. At about this time, around 1636, the Stadtholder Frederick Henry commissioned a series of paintings depicting scenes from the Passion. This important commission seems to have been obtained for Rembrandt by Constantijn Huygens, with whom he kept up a correspondence on the subject which lasted until 1639.

But already the artist's life was clouded by sorrow and difficulties. Of the four children born to Saskia, only the last, Titus, survived: their first child, Rumbartus, and two daughters both called Cornelia, born respectively in 1635, 1638 and 1640, all died in infancy. In 1638 Rembrandt was forced to bring a law suit against members of Saskia's family, who were publicly accusing him of dissipating her dowry. However, he did not let these difficulties affect his work, nor did his market value decline; in fact, it was about this time that copies of his paintings began to circulate, as can be seen from the inventory of the possessions of Cornelius Aertszoon, a merchant, drawn up on 7 May 1637. Moreover, by about 1640, some of his paintings had been acquired by Charles I of England.

In January 1639, Rembrandt purchased from one Christoffel Thijssens, for the vast sum of 13,000 florins, a large and luxurious house in the St Anthoniesbreestraat. (The street was later renamed Jodenbreestraat, and the house now serves as the Rembrandthuis Museum.) He undertook to pay off this sum in yearly instalments, and moved there on 1 May. He spent the next few years embellishing his new home. Collections of curiosities were very common at this time, and Rembrandt's taste differed from that of his contemporaries only in an even stronger emphasis upon what was bizarre or quaint. It was in this house that Rembrandt set up his studio, which was attended by an ever-growing number of young apprentices and pupils, who submitted themselves to the severe discipline he imposed. According to Arnold Houbraken, the author of a work (1718) on Dutch painters, in order to accommodate all his pupils, Rembrandt rented a warehouse as well, where he divided the room into small cubicles, by means of 'simple curtains or paper partitions, so that they could work freely from life, without disturbing each other.'

Rembrandt was completely engrossed in his work and there was little place in his life for even the smallest pleasures: at table, wrote Houbraken, 'he contented himself with a piece of bread and cheese or a herring'; at the same time, according to the same source, 'his works were so sought after that people had to wait their turn for a long time and, in the words of the proverb, they had not only to pay him, but to pray him.' The first biography of Rembrandt was published in 1641 by Johannes Orlers, and his paintings became known and sought after in Paris. His interest in art dealing was still strong. He became co-owner, with the dealer Pieter de la Tombe, of *The Samaritan Woman*, attributed to Giorgione, and of Palma Vecchio's *Rich Man*. At the sale of the Lucas van Uffelen collection, he was interested in buying Raphael's *Portrait of Castiglione*, but was forestalled by Alfonso Lopez, who bought it on behalf of Richelieu; so he made a rapid copy of it. We do not know to what extent he was in touch with the cultural and religious circles of Amsterdam (although it is known that he did have connexions with the Mennonites), nor how far he had maintained contact with the university world of Leyden.

On 14 September 1641 Rembrandt's mother died in Leyden; on 14 June 1642 his beloved Saskia died, nine months after the birth of their son Titus. On 19 July he bought her a tomb, in the Oude Kerk in Amsterdam. He continued to work despite his grief, and in the same year, 1642, completed one of his most striking paintings, *The Parade of the Civic Guard under Captain F. Banning Cocq*, usually known as *The Night Watch*. It is probable that Rembrandt's original treatment of portraiture and colour was beginning to disconcert and disturb his circles of patrons. In a letter to Huygens, written as early as January 1639, he stated that his intention was to express 'the utmost in naturalness and action'; later, he proudly described himself as 'a painter, not a dyer.'

In 1643, Rembrandt took into his household a certain Geertge Dircx, a trumpeter's widow, as nurse to Titus. They soon formed an attachment, and continued to live together until 1648. However, a year later the relationship suddenly ended, when Geertge brought a suit against Rembrandt for breach of promise. He was summoned before the Matrimonial Court, but sent someone in his place to testify that he had never promised marriage. A settlement was reached on 14 October 1649, providing for Geertge's departure, but nevertheless ordering Rembrandt to pay her a pension of 200 florins a year. (She died not long afterwards in an asylum.)

It is at this time, 1649, that Rembrandt's biographers first mention Hendrickje Stoffels, 'a servant girl, aged twenty-three.' She seems to have won Rembrandt's deep affection, and she remained with him, his wife in all but name, until her death in 1663. (They could never marry, for, by the terms of Saskia's will, Rembrandt would have forfeited half the estate if he had remarried – a financial loss he could simply not afford.) Their relationship was disturbed only by outside interference: because of its obvious irregularity, it incurred not only the disapproval of the neighbours, but the severity of the law. In 1654 Rembrandt and Hendrickje were several times summoned by the Council of the Reformed Church to answer the charge of concubinage; they ignored the summons. Finally, Hendrickje appeared before the court, and admitted the relationship. She was severely admonished for her licentious conduct, and was urged to have Cornelia, her natural child by Rembrandt, baptized.

The baptism took place in the Oude Kerk on 30 October 1654; the couple continued to live in sin.

Rembrandt's commercial success had declined rapidly during these years (in a sale held at Delft in 1650, one of his paintings went for only 60 florins), and he was in serious financial difficulties. By 1653 he was facing complete ruin: he was in arrears with payments on his house in the Breestraat and in debt to several people, including Jan Six, who had been not only his closest friend but a patron. He made a last-minute bid to save the situation by transferring the deeds of the house to Titus's name, but the attempt failed. His creditors foreclosed, and he was declared bankrupt. On 25 and 26 July 1656, an inventory was made of all his possessions in the house in the Breestraat. His belongings were auctioned, for very low prices, between 4 December 1658 and January 1659 at the Keyserskroon, an inn at which he was temporarily living.

A period of great hardship now began, although Rembrandt – who meanwhile had moved with his family to a small house on the Rozengracht – was absorbed in his work as never before. He could not sell his works, since he was no longer allowed to carry on any form of trade in the city. However, in December 1660, in order to get round the difficulty, Hendrickje and Titus set up a company for art dealing, under the terms of which Rembrandt became their employee, and handed over to them all his new works in exchange for food and lodging. No concrete improvements resulted from this arrangement, and further suffering and disappointment followed. But at least Rembrandt must have been comforted by the unfailing support that Hendrickje and Titus gave him in these years, and his dedication to his work remained unaffected. On 7 August 1661, Hendrickje, who was ill, went to the notary to make her will: she left her property to Cornelia, with the provision that everything would revert to Titus if Cornelia died childless. Hendrickje struggled on for two more years; she died in July 1663, when she was still in her thirties.

In the summer of 1662, the city fathers of Amsterdam rejected Rembrandt's *Conspiracy of Julius Civilis*, although it had been painted on commission for the newly rebuilt

*The Conspiracy of Julius Civilis (see p. 39)*

town hall. In October 1662, he was so short of money that he had to sell Saskia's tomb in the Oude Kerk. Titus became of age and free of his guardians in 1665. On 10 February 1668, he married Magdalena van Loo; seven months later he died. His daughter, Titia, was born posthumously in March 1669.

The end, for Rembrandt too, was close at hand: the records of the Westerkerk contain the entry referring to the death, on Tuesday, 4 October 1669, of 'Rembrandt van Rijn, painter, in the Rozengracht, opposite the Doelhof. Leaves two children.' (Since Cornelia was his only surviving child, the second child to which the entry refers is probably his grand-daughter Titia.) 'This painter and engraver,' wrote Baldinucci in 1686, 'was very different from other men in the government of himself... he looked down on everyone. As for his appearance, his ugly and plebeian face was accompanied by untidy and dirty clothes, for it was his custom, when at work, to wipe his brushes on himself, and to do other things of a similar nature. When he was working he would not have granted an audience to the first Monarch of the World, who would have had to come back, and come back again, until he found him unoccupied.'

# Works

Eugène Fromentin, in his *Maîtres d'autrefois* (1877), suggested the way to approach Rembrandt's art: 'It is difficult to isolate it from the intellectual and moral climate of his time, since the very air he breathed was the air of the Dutch seventeenth century into which he was born. Had he come earlier, he would have been inexplicable; had he been born elsewhere, no matter where, he would have fulfilled the role attributed to him, that of a comet moving outside the sphere of modern art, in an even more singular fashion; had he come later, he would no longer have had the immense merit of ending an epoch while opening one of the great doors to the future.'

Scholars have often lamented the relative lack of precise information about Rembrandt – information which might have thrown light on certain vital aspects of his life and personality and thus provided a useful means of interpreting his painting. In certain periods, this lack of precision encouraged the myth of Rembrandt as a 'magnificent, sad painter', lonely and withdrawn from the outside world, wholly preoccupied with his own visions. This myth is current in the writings of some biographers of the romantic school, and even today finds adherents. Fromentin himself could not help speculating about Rembrandt's education, whether it covered at least the reading of certain obvious books, as would seem likely in view of his sense of the theatre and his interest in history, mythology and Christian dogma; on the other hand, the almost complete absence of books in the inventories of his possessions suggests that this was not the case. It is, in addition, very difficult to determine the quality of his philosophical interests, or to what extent he was involved in the political, religious and social problems which troubled Holland at this time.

The most serious gap, however, Fromentin writes regretfully, is that we know nothing about his feelings: 'Saskia dies, but his work continues without a day's interruption; we know from the dating of his pictures and, even better, of his etchings, that this was so. His fortune crumbles, he is brought before the bankruptcy court, all that he holds dear is taken from him: he carries away his easel, moves to another place, and neither his contemporaries nor posterity have heard a single cry or lament from this strange character, whom one would have expected to have been completely prostrated. His activity does not lose impetus or grow less. Patronage, fortune, happiness and wealth abandon him: he answers the injustice of fate, the fickleness of the public with . . . some of his most resolute, convinced and vigorous works.'

The fact is that to understand Rembrandt's personality one must relate it to the precise time and place in which he lived, and to the severe bourgeois morality of his social class. He takes his place as a member of a society which Fromentin describes as 'a nation of bourgeois, practical, undisposed to dreaming, busy about their affairs, having nothing of the mystic in their nature, anti-Latin in spirit, with broken traditions, a prosaic religion and parsimonious habits.' Rembrandt once wrote – in 1634, in the autograph album of the German traveller Burchard Grossmann – 'An upright heart puts honour before wealth'. His choice of this motto is significant. As a producer of works of art, and as an art dealer, he had to concern himself with giving his patrons not only aesthetic pleasure but a safe investment. In this approach to his work, which was determined by the economic structure of the country, he merely reflected the attitude towards labour and reward which was shared alike by the businessmen and artisans, the bourgeois and petty-bourgeois, who were a fundamental element in Dutch seventeenth-century society. It was an attitude of 'lay asceticism', Calvinistic in origin, and has been best described by Max Weber in his famous study of the relationship between the Protestant ethic and capitalism.

At the root of this attitude there was to be found, if not an actual disdain for or indifference to accumulated wealth, a certain detachment arising from the awareness that such wealth has been granted by the Grace of God and man is only its administrator. On the other hand, as Weber said, 'in the sphere of the production of wealth, bourgeois asceticism stood up against dishonesty and purely impulsive greed ', insisting on a profound and incorruptible probity in work: in other words, honour before wealth. It should be added that this tendency was the most apparent among those classes whose social status was not yet fully established in the economic order – especially the class to which Rembrandt owed his origins, that of the petty-bourgeoisie. The ideology of probity and honour was proclaimed by the various religious sects to which these classes traditionally belonged, including the Mennonites, with whom we know that Rembrandt was linked.

As we have seen, when Huygens visited Rembrandt and Lievens in their Leyden studio in about 1630, he was deeply impressed by the young men's total dedication to their work; and, similarly, Baldinucci (1686) could not help marvelling at their total absorption in their art, and their indifference to any pressure put upon them by their patrons, of whatever social rank. Nothing but work interested Rembrandt, and he was wholly dedicated to his art; but at the same time he avoided the pitfalls of the academic tradition, including the ' compulsory' journey to Italy. He rejected Huygens's suggestion that he should make this journey, and was blamed both by Joachim von Sandrart, the German painter and art historian, and by Baldinucci for not heeding his advice. ' All he lacks is to have visited Italy ', lamented Sandrart in his *Academia Tedesca* (1675), ' and those places where one can learn to know the masters of antiquity and the theory of art.' Sandrart then goes on to show his complete lack of understanding of the ascetic nature (in the sense indicated above) of Rembrandt's attitude to work, and at the same time records his amazement at the artist's rejection of all academic influences and his tranquil acceptance of his place as an ordinary member of a society. To a man like Sandrart, it seemed incredible that Rembrandt should not wish to cultivate connexions at court and among the circles of the nobility – circles which carried great prestige and must surely ennoble the position of the artist in society.

Thus Rembrandt must be seen as being firmly wedded to his social class and to his country: he travelled little, and then only within the boundaries of Holland, particularly between Leyden and Amsterdam, and possibly not at all after 1640. The following remarks made by his pupil Hoogstraten, who was very close to him, are revealing. When Hoogstraten's brother said that he wanted to make the *voyage d'Italie*, Hoogstraten replied: ' You will find so many beautiful things in your own country that your life will be too short to understand and express them. However beautiful Italy may be, it will avail you nothing if you are incapable of expressing the nature you have around you. ' In these words he was probably echoing advice that he must have heard many times from his master.

The Holland of Rembrandt did not come into being as an independent entity until 1609, after the violent struggle of the northern provinces (Zeeland, Gelderland, Utrecht, Friesland, Drenthe) against Spanish oppression. The struggle involved the southern regions as well, although their aspirations to freedom remained unfulfilled. The structure of the state was constituted in an unusual manner, as regards both its economic foundations and its social and political organization. It was a confederation of cities, whose growing prosperity had begun some decades earlier, on the basis of their historical and geographical positions, and rested mainly upon their activities of commerce and navigation. The type of administration adopted by these cities was medieval, incorporating, for example, the old guilds, which had remained intact throughout the centuries. It was a type of organization which proved extremely effective in the particular circumstances of the Dutch seventeenth century. It became possible to overcome particular interests and bring a bitter collective struggle to a victorious conclusion because it was seen that this was a matter of survival; after success had been achieved, the same reason led to the creation of a ' decentralized ' state around the House of Orange, which had led the movement towards independence.

The most striking feature of the new state was the delicate balance among the individual communities, as they stood firm against any tendency to create a centrifugal organization. At the same time, the struggle resulted in the birth of a genuine popular national consciousness, and when religious conflicts later tore Europe apart, Holland was able to make a unanimous choice in favour of the reformed faith, thus holding new weapons, ideological this time, to be used against her Catholic adversaries. The corporative form of Holland's economic system meant that the control of wealth was in the hands not of the state or a dynasty, but of the merchant bourgeoisie, who thus became the dominant class and wielded political power. At the summit of this system, acting more or less as its moderator, was the Stadtholder, who held certain sovereign rights; next to him came the Grand Pensioner, who acted as Secretary of State. One great advantage of the system was that there were no rigid class demarcations, and hence no serious forms of oppression of one class by another. Thus, corresponding to the ' horizontal ' equilibrium among the municipal centres of the ' United Provinces ', there was a ' vertical ' equilibrium in class relationships – in short, a ' social amalgam ', to use the term coined by Johan Huizinga in his invaluable study (1941).

The factors contributing to this situation are complex, and go far beyond the awakening of a national consciousness, which was able to settle all the internal conflicts of society. Other important factors included the concrete availability of wealth, which had become diverted from investment in land and the accumulation of inert capital and became redeployed in commerce and production. This created an advantageous situation for the lower classes, who could now be sure of obtaining employment and could themselves attain a position of comfort. At the same time, the aristocracy of feudal and peasant origin (with the exception of the politically unimportant foreign aristocracy of the eastern regions, who formed a closed society) tended to form matrimonial ties with the urban middle class and to participate in their mercantile activity. Finally, the reformed spirit of religion not only provided a reflection of this structure of society in the realm of ideology, but also proved to be a vital element in cementing the ' social amalgam '. This process did not lose momentum until

English competition made itself felt, especially after Cromwell's Navigation Act of 1651, which dealt a hard blow to Dutch mercantile expansion on the seas and led to an alteration in the relationship between the production of wealth and the social strata, and, as will be seen, to an inevitable modification of the customs and attitudes of the establishment.

Against this background, culture – which includes our field of special interest, the visual arts – was not seen as the exclusive privilege of the class which held real power. 'However strange it may seem', remarks Huizinga (1941), 'the production of the goods of the spirit was not linked except in a limited degree to certain classes or economic conditions', so that a wide area of society participated actively in the cultural process, both as producers and as consumers. In a Europe conditioned by the Counter-Reformation and inclined towards absolutism, the word 'culture' had a distinctly bourgeois connotation, so that individuality or originality was limited to that extent. The part played by painting was of particular importance in Dutch society, where the absence of ecclesiastical influence (as a class, the clergy does not exist in Holland) and the lack of interest in the investment of wealth in land and property limited the growth of a solid tradition of architecture or sculpture (and, for this reason also, limited the possibilities for artists to produce large decorative compositions). Small easel paintings were in constant demand for private houses (as were etchings, both as works of art in their own right and as reproductions) in all social classes, almost to the exclusion of all other types of art. These easel paintings, together with other furnishings of the home, satisfied a need for comfort and, as Weber believed, enlarged the scope of what it was morally permissible to spend money on. They corresponded to the ideal of what private middle-class citizens wanted in the ordered and secure comfort of their homes, while at the same time providing a means of investing their often excessive liquid capital.

Among those who provided culture, the painters, whose works were in great demand, formed a numerous body.

Their place in society was usually quite modest, not compa-
rable, for example, with that of writers or poets, since the
profession of artists was exercised among the ranks of the
small craftsmen, who were even more sensitive to the
concept of 'asceticism' in work than their colleagues in
other fields. The very nature of their position and historical
role excluded any academic or intellectual emphasis in
their painting, such as characterized the Renaissance and
post-Renaissance tradition of the south and the circles of
the court, and ultimately excluded also the possibility of
their attaining social positions of prestige or importance.
When one traces the origins of artists, one nearly always
finds that they come from the lower middle class or from
families of modest means. In these circumstances, 'the
subject of art became first and foremost that which was
the property of the individual, of the family, of the com-
munity or the nation: the room and the corridor, the house
and courtyard, the city and its surroundings, the native
landscape and the liberated and redeemed fatherland, but
also the individual himself, the family group or the corporative group of the guild'; as a result, 'the more up-to-
date, obvious and everyday a subject, the greater its value
to art' (H. Hauser, 1927). Objectivity and realism, ensured
by the artist's direct experience and participation, became
the mode of expression in art of the firmly held bourgeois
ideal of the 'everyday', an anti-classical ideal which perme-
ated every strata of the 'social amalgam'.
Rembrandt emerges as the great poet of that society. He
knew how to live in it, and to interpret it with the visionary
(in the concrete, not generic and vague, sense of the term)
force of his genius. He took as his own that which was
peculiar to that society, and, by transforming it through
the incomparable medium of his art, created a universal
work. As H. Focillon (1935) points out, Rembrandt not
only illustrates, but invents, Holland. He was able to
understand the spirit of Holland – a country enjoying a
period of security and wealth – and could, 'as no other
artist has done before him, state clearly the problem of
the relationship between man and the universe, between
the creative artist and his time, between style and subject

matter .' But, for this reason, one cannot in any sense regard him as a painter of the intangible, an evoker of fantasies, since ' no artist has observed appearances more closely, none has ever possessed a surer and more vigorous hand in probing the matters of this world. '

Biographers agree that Rembrandt's apprenticeship with Van Swanenburgh in 1621-3 can have been no more than an introduction to his profession. We know from the few existing examples of Van Swanenburgh's work that he had very little to teach, even though he had followed the usual practice of travelling to Italy: he was an artist of little talent, whose technique was poor and uninspired. Of far greater significance was Rembrandt's move to Amsterdam in 1624, when he worked in the studio of Pieter Lastman. Lastman, too, had taken the compulsory journey to Italy, and had become a great admirer of Caravaggio and Adam Elsheimer, whose work he saw in Rome. He was deeply impressed by the use of light in the paintings of these two artists, but never mastered the lesson himself. His works, a series of historical paintings on mythological and sacred themes, remained, for the most part, highly conventional.

In the first works produced by Rembrandt, dating from about 1625, he followed his master's example, even to his choice of subjects. (It was in Lastman's studio that Rembrandt developed his taste for biblical themes – a taste to which he remained faithful for the rest of his life.) Thus, such paintings as *The Stoning of St Stephen* in the Musée des Beaux-Arts, Lyon, or *The Justice of Brutus* in the Stadelijck Museum, Leyden, painted in 1625-6, form part of a pictorial tradition which, although it has been brought up to date in some certain stylistic respects, belongs generally to the Italian school; in other words, it is entirely foreign to those national currents which were at the time leading to an interest in portraiture and landscape – in short, to a naturalistic portrayal of reality.

The years 1627-30, however, saw a progressive and increasingly marked evolution in Rembrandt's art. Although he continued to paint historical subjects, especially subjects taken from the Scriptures, he was becoming more and more interested in reality, and began to experiment with the possibilities of light as a means of emphasizing the most significant element in a story. This finally resulted in reducing the importance of the framework of the composition and concentrating entirely on the passages of real interest: in other words, light was withdrawn from the formal elements in the composition and made to fall on certain significant images. A restless dynamism invaded the painting, expressing the world of the emotions as it is mirrored in the appearance of reality. *Judas returning the thirty pieces of silver*, dated 1629, in the Marquess of Normandy collection, Mulgrove Castle, Whitby, is a work which demonstrates Rembrandt's now irreversible emphasis on the emotions and the attainment of a style which could already meet the high demand put on it. As Focillon (1935) points out, to speak of 'chiaroscuro', and leave it at that, is, in fact, to say very little. There is a world of difference, Focillon continues, 'between the graceful Chinese shadows of Elsheimer, the Italian work of Caravaggio, who amuses himself, like a skilful stage producer, in " machinations " of the action from below ground level, and finally, the slow planetary gravitation of the patient faces of Georges de La Tour, painted around a flower-like flame.'

It was about this time that Rembrandt began to adopt subjects explicitly linked with daily life and to concentrate on portraiture. Even when he painted historical subjects, which he continued to do all his life, the feeling of everyday reality was always present. These historical subjects thus came to be seen in a new light, being reinterpreted by the artist and made to represent a concrete, contemporary psychological situation. The radical, anticlassical attitude which Rembrandt had inherited from his bourgeois origins now made itself felt. The classical concept of form – a static abstraction of certain ideal aspects of life, constituting a super-world outside the process of daily life – ceased to interest him. What interested him now was form as the expression of the process of living.

Rembrandt's attitude is most clearly demonstrated by his treatment of the portrait. From the very beginning, in works painted about 1629-30, he never used the portrait as a device for portraying a type, but as a means of penetrating the personality of the sitter, of expressing it as it was at an unrepeatable psychological moment in his life and as it was reflected in his features. The concept of beauty of form thus ceased to apply, and in the artist's effort to grasp the interaction of spirit and flesh which alone interested him, life itself conquered and overcame beauty. Rembrandt's tendency to do several portraits of the same person corresponded to his desire to express the process of life over a period of time, showing how the character of his sitter varied, not only physiologically but spiritually, as his external circumstances changed. Since character varies at given moments in a person's existence (although, of course, each successive moment contains within itself those which have preceded it), Rembrandt could in this way clarify what is meant when one speaks of a person's identity. This diversity appears in his portraits in the form of a particular expression, a certain gesture, which indicates and 'portrays' the individual pattern of every personal destiny, just as light, falling on a glance, a face or a hand arrests and fixes for ever a moment of joy or sorrow, meditation or abandon.

Rembrandt continued his experimentation in technique with untiring perseverance, endeavouring to make it a flexible instrument, able to express all that he required of it. Baldinucci provides the following illuminating description of the artist's technique: 'His manner of painting was most odd, and he created a style which, it could be said, was entirely his own, using no outlines, either internal or external, but doing everything by rough stabs, applied with great force but without depth. And what is almost impossible to understand is how, painting in stabs, he could work so slowly and labour so long and so hard ... As soon as the first stage of the work was completed, he went back over it with new stabs, and little strokes, until the colour sometimes stood up at such points to a depth of almost half an inch; so that one can say of him that he worked always, taking no rest.' André Félibien (1685), too, had already spoken of Rembrandt's tendency to 'use great brush strokes, and to apply the colours very thickly, without mixing or softening them.' These comments are interesting in the light of two statements that Rembrandt himself is reported to have made: that a work is to be considered completed when the artist has said all he had to say, and that he considered himself a painter, not a dyer.

In *The Presentation in the Temple*, one version (1631) of which is in the Mauritshuis, The Hague, Rembrandt turned to a favourite subject in historical painting. It was a complex work, owing to the large number of participants in the action and the need to set the stage for a monumental representation. From the ideal centre of the composition, which is here the same as the actual centre, the light rises and radiates in all directions, before it fades into the mysterious shadows which all but mask the faces of the spectators who crowd the staircase and line of pillars. The pillars are magnified by means of tonal graduation, which has been created by scratching away the grey-green colour of the second layer of paint. Indeed, the surrounding space comes into being, as Baldinucci said, with 'no outlines, either internal or external', but by this calculated tonal graduation, resulting in the interdependence of every element in the composition. Space here is not a fixed part of the composition into which the action has to be fitted; rather, space and action are one and the same. By bringing out all the expressive possibilities of his theme, Rembrandt has brought it onto a poetic plane. The development of his technique made this possible: light no longer serves to isolate moments of 'truth' from the formless and disquieting chaos of darkness and night, but has become part of a dialogue in which light and shade interpenetrate and integrate with each other, each in turn modifying the other so that there is no division between them.

For Rembrandt, there was no fundamental metaphysical contrast or dualism between the diverse spheres of reality. Hence we do not find in his works the tragic conception of life expressed, for example, in the literature of France at that period – a country whose quite different historical structure had resulted in profound social upheavals. As Simmel (1919) points out, Rembrandt's treatment of light 'informs' the ebb and flow of existence, in its full diversity, and one aspect cannot be dissociated from the rest; it therefore follows that the formal unity of the image 'is woven immediately from the varied forms of animation seen in the characters in the painting' and is, in fact, due solely to the 'co-operation of purely personal spheres ... without friction, since the figures are equal in spirit.' This harmony between figures and background can be seen again in *St Anastasius* (*pl. 2*), a painting which, like the *Presentation in the Temple*, dates from 1631.

Concerned above all to achieve expressiveness, Rembrandt had developed by this stage a technique which was entirely adequate to meet the demands made upon it. He now turned to the traditional subject of the group portrait, but his manner of treating it was revolutionary both in spirit and in the arrangement of the composition. In the tradition of Dutch seventeenth-century art, the group portrait represented what one might call a typological module, whose origins and development clearly belonged to the co-operative structure of the country's society: it was intended to be a static representation of the members of the various guilds, showing them in the way they would wish to be remembered by those who came after them. Apart from these official portraits, there were almost no other public commissions for artists. Owing to the well-defined tradition of group portraiture, it was generally understood that the artist called upon to execute it had to respect the rigorous rules applying to the arrangement and position of the sitters. Rembrandt's first work in the *genre, The Anatomy lesson of Professor Tulp* (*pls 3-6*), departs from this rigid typological formula and treats the subject in an entirely new way.

In this painting, executed in 1632, Rembrandt ignores all previous models, in which the static arrangement of the figures had followed a hierarchic pattern according to their position within the corporation, and in which the corpse would have appeared in the picture merely as an emblem of the guild and in order to justify the association of this particular collection of individuals to form a group, while a strong diffused light falling on the static figures ranged round the corpse would have given them prominence and flattered them. Rembrandt, by contrast, instinctively seizes

21

upon the most dramatic elements in the scene; he expresses the different reactions of those present, which vary both in manner and in intensity, and brings them together into a unified work of dynamic tension, which is at the same time compressed and co-ordinated. The light falls upon the corpse, which is the focal point of the composition, and emphasizes the red network of tendons which the surgeon's scalpel exposes to his students' view. The figure of the professor stands alone on one side of the corpse, and the light reflects on the faces and gestures of the surgeon and his students in such a way as to reveal their personalities and capture them for ever at an unrepeatable moment in their lives. What is by its nature a transitory event has become fixed and has been made permanent through the inner process of the personality of each participant.

Although Rembrandt's treatment of this subject was so obviously contrary to the conventions – but certainly without any explicit intention on his part – it did not arouse the hostility or dissent of his patrons or the public. On the contrary, the painting enjoyed great success and increased the demand for his works. This success encouraged him to stand firm by his methods and not to try to follow convention. The firmness and constancy with which he kept to his chosen path sprang from the spirit of artisan morality – of ‘honour’, as he himself expressed it – which was inherent in the class of society to which he belonged. The same spirit prevailed whether his subject was the portrait of a group, a single figure or two figures. Wherever possible he portrayed his sitters in a natural situation, often engaged in conversation, and he refused to flatter them. In the historical paintings of biblical or mythological subjects, he sought out the significant moment in the drama and made it appear alive and up to date. Even the painting of landscape became a pretext for depicting the artist's state of mind, sometimes calm, sometimes troubled (*pls 9-11*).

This was a very fertile period in Rembrandt's art, especially following his meeting with Saskia and during the happy years of their marriage. His paintings at this time were variations on the themes of his happiness in requited love, his joy in life, his entirely earthly delight in flesh. There were a series of self-portraits and double portraits with Saskia in which they often appear 'disguised' in the most extraordinary and unlikely costumes, as in the celebrated *Self-portrait with Saskia* (*pl. 8*). At other times, mythological subjects, such as *Susanna bathing*, in the Mauritshuis, The Hague, or *Danaë* (*pls 13-15*), became a pretext for more portraits of Saskia, at moments of intimacy and happy abandon.

Huizinga (1941) criticized Rembrandt for his fondness for 'disguise' in portraits and for historical subjects, and saw in this predilection a limitation of the artist's genius, since it seemed to imply a wish to render a world and a form of existence different from that of everyday life; this, Huizinga felt, could lead to a 'magniloquent style' and a 'striving for monumentality and classical harmony'. In fact, the elements of fantasy which Rembrandt incorporated in his paintings never betray his prime concern for realism (a realism which, however, does not degenerate into a banal naturalism), for the portrayal of a psychological state or conflict in a concrete situation. Sometimes these elements of fantasy were used to counterpoint, to give greater vigour to, an image, or else they could be employed to stress the significance of a given event. Far from seeking escape in some impossible dream of classicism and grandeur, Rembrandt tries to express an objective psychological truth – in all its aspects – in the illusory world that is painting. His statement, already quoted, that a painting is to be considered finished when the artist has said all he had to say, not only explains his tenacity, but helps us to understand why he incorporated the most unlikely elements in his art.

Rembrandt's attitude to Italian art, based on works that came up for sale on the Dutch market or on engravings, is significant: he was concerned with one thing only, the opportunity these works provided for 'testing' certain formal arrangements and methods which he could relate to his own ideas, while rejecting *ipso facto* the classical structure of that form. Italian art certainly proved a stimulus to him and aroused his enthusiastic admiration, but that was as far as he went; for a classical painting (and the term must be taken to include also the painting of the mannerist school, which did not reject the formal values of classical art, but distorted them for its own ends) presupposes a process of abstraction and idealization, and a denial of the everyday world, which was alien to Rembrandt's nature.

Writing about the Louvre *Bathsheba* (*pl. 57*), one of Rembrandt's late works, Focillon declared (1935): 'Through her whole body there breathes the enchanting intimacy of everyday life, transported into the quiet areas and shadows of the painted figures. Her flesh is no stranger to toil, but has the weight and softness, the fullness of living matter, not something taken out of a theoretical treatise.'

Even when Rembrandt adopted iconographic formulas, which he took from various sources, he incorporated them in such a manner that they became quite different in his hands. That he adhered to the religious beliefs of the Reformation is beyond doubt, yet it remains very difficult to define his personal ideology from the scanty information we possess. Certainly the Lutheran concept that prayer is of less value than action and good works, according to each person's position in society, comprised a reappraisal of the importance of the things of daily life of which he cannot have been unaware. But there was a certain duality in the Lutheran attitude to good works, with its assumption that by performing such works one would earn the reward of beatitude, which does not seem to fit in with what we know about Rembrandt. For him, there never existed a sense of dissociation between the 'here and now' and the 'beyond', with the necessity for choice and the anguish such a distinction entails.

One fact, at least, seems certain, and that is Rembrandt's acceptance into the sect of the Mennonites, which must have helped to form his vision of the universe. This sect, wrote Baldinucci, lived in a strange way: 'Their clergy are not chosen among the educated, but they appoint to this office men of low condition, whom they esteem and whom we would call Worthy and Just Men, and for the rest they live as they please.' And Adriaes Pels, a compatriot of Rembrandt's, wrote a poem in which he criticizes the painter in a manner which seems to confirm that he was a participating member of a movement, such as that of the Mennonites, which believed in religious subjectivism and was just as rebellious towards the established Calvinist church as it was to all confessional institutions: 'The more the spirit has raised itself, the more will it be lost – if it does not abide by principles and rules, but claims to know everything for itself.'

Other hypotheses which have been put forward are much less convincing: that Rembrandt frequented groups of educated French Calvinist exiles or, as W. R. Valentiner believes (1957), that he held beliefs akin to the pantheism later propounded by Spinoza. Whether we accept Valentiner's argument or not, there is certainly some analogy – in form, if nothing else – between Rembrandt's view of life and Spinoza's conception of God as the cause of all things, a cause which is not external to them, but lies within, so that all things are merely modifications of the substance of God. This is illustrated by Rembrandt's radical tendency never to put one aspect of life above any other – choosing some, discarding others – but to penetrate all things as they manifest themselves in their day-to-day existence, and to capture the spiritual quality of his sitters as an intrinsic and inseparable part of their existence in the here and now.

A detailed analysis of the works painted by Rembrandt after 1636-7 is not possible within the scope of this study (just as, for space reasons, consideration of his graphic art has been omitted altogether). By this time Rembrandt was concerned not so much to develop his style and technique as to stretch to the utmost the techniques he had already evolved, in an incessant struggle to do justice to his subjects and to his inexhaustible imagination and vitality (*pls 16-24*). In 1642, he painted another group portrait, one of his most revolutionary works: *The Parade of the Civic Guard under Captain F. Banning Cocq*, which came to be known as *The Night Watch* (*pls 25-32*). Again, this painting defied the rigid rules laid down for group portraiture, which were intended to result in a 'memorable' portrayal of the main figure in the scene, with the rest of the composition fulfilling a subordinate function; according to this formula, the captain would have stood out prominently among his guards, who would all have been standing rigidly to attention. Rembrandt rejected such an arrangement out of hand, and instead took as his setting the moment of excitement and confusion when the guards form ranks at their captain's orders: in other words, as L. Münz (1952) has observed, he chose to arrest the fleeting moment, and from the dynamic interplay of the individual personalities was able to create an authentic corporate unit. His bold use of colour, displayed here in brilliant phantasmagoria, provided a perfect vehicle for such an undertaking. As Münz says, seen at close range, the painting appears to be a formless chaos of contrasting light and colour effects; but from a distance the individual elements stand out from each other distinctly, while at the same time merging to form a well-ordered composition.

The composition is created, reconstructed and then broken up, to come into being again, in a constant process of dynamic interplay. This is achieved through the simultaneous use of the most varied techniques (even so early a critic as Félibien had remarked on the idiosyncratic manner of Rembrandt's painting): expanses of flat colour placed alongside hasty and urgent brush-strokes; the addition of layer upon layer of colour, applied with a spatula and then scratched off to reveal the lower surfaces in greater light; thin, almost transparent, glazes. We are reminded of how Baldinucci described Rembrandt's technique as one of 'rough stabs', and how he found it hard to reconcile this method with the fact that he 'worked so slowly and laboured so long'.

*The Night Watch* was conceived and carried to completion during the tense days of the illness and death of Saskia; as noted, Fromentin remarked on the detachment Rembrandt showed in the face of this family tragedy, not permitting any interruption to his work. The painting is a point both of arrival and of departure in the history of Rembrandt's art; when looking at it, one can understand how he came to be described as a latter-day Titian, Tintoretto or

Bassano the Elder – painters whose phantasmagoria of colours led the Renaissance into a catastrophic dissolution of form. There is no doubt that in this masterpiece Rembrandt defied all the conventions of the local tradition of portraiture in order to be free to express his personal vision of reality in his own way. His world becomes charged with violence and challenge – a challenge which could be met only by the honest, craftsman-like attitude of the artist, in his determination to express what he wishes to say up to the limit, without hesitations or concessions, and to transfer his vision on to the canvas without any loss of immediacy or integrity.

It seems probable that Rembrandt's patrons did not take kindly to this flouting of the conventions, but their disapproval did not have immediate repercussions. These occurred later, as a result of the crisis in the Dutch economy which was brought about by the Navigation Act and the inevitable social effects which followed. Class distinctions became more rigid – to look ahead for a moment – and the first bankruptcies took place: the wealthy middle class tended, on the one hand, to take their capital away from investment and put it to more profitable use and, on the other hand, to consolidate more firmly their control of political power. People's way of life – again to look ahead – their tastes and habits, were affected and altered: the arts were required to fulfil new functions, in conformity with a classicist ideal of decorum.

In the works Rembrandt painted after 1642 (*pls 33-43, 40-42*), the illusionistic effects contained in *The Night Watch* continued to reflect his determined effort to express psychological reality. This remained a constant goal with him however greatly the subjects of the paintings might differ: Old and New Testament stories, or portraits, which were now usually of a single figure. Similarly, whether the technique was that of oil painting or etching, the possibilities of the medium were explored to the full, with an incredible range of treatment. Some of the most striking portraits are those painted around 1645 and after (*pls 39, 43-48, 51*); they show an important development in the artist's relationship to his model, ' an attitude revealing an amazing strength, gentleness and truth' according to Roger de Piles (1699). Rembrandt's effort to penetrate the individual life of his sitter, in order to express the reality of one moment out of the sum of moments which make up a person's life and in this way to 'represent' the existence of each person in his inimitable individuality, had enabled him also to become aware of the destiny of his sitter: the death which lurks behind every moment of life and is the inevitable end of every personality. As A. Banfi (1926) puts it: 'Life always carries within itself the negative moment of death ... not as a matter of external chance, an event whose accidental nature contrasts strangely with the inescapable universality of life, but as an internal destiny, the necessary pole to the rhythm of life itself.' Rembrandt now observed that the people he was studying 'carried their term within themselves ... and the negative side of life was inside them'; in other words, he became aware of the inner nature of death, and made it his task to seek out and portray 'the mysterious mark of death in the living.'

This 'discovery', however, did not disturb or shatter Rembrandt's unified vision of the universe, in the sense of a metaphysical 'break', since an awareness of death was the result of meditation on life and love of life. Rather, he came to see death as a complementary aspect of life, containing its ultimate significance and setting the seal upon it. The metaphors generally applied to death – a broken thread, a jump into the abyss, a leap in the dark, a passageway to the unknown – become irrelevant. According to one definition, tragedy is based on an ideology which affirms man's powerlessness to create on earth a life which is valid. In this sense, for Rembrandt, death always remains this side of tragedy, since such an ideology is quite alien to his perception of the world and man's historical role in it. The effect of his new awareness of death was not to introduce anguish and torment into his art: rather, it gave him profounder powers to express psychological truth. In seizing and fixing the image, he was able to express also the sense of individual destiny, seen as a whole, from the beginning to the end of his sitter's life. In this way, his art brought a sense of the totality of experience, resolved the religiosity of the practical, middle-class civilization of Holland. It represented the ultimate act of awareness, carrying the notion of daily reality to its extreme limits.

Also at this period, Rembrandt's palette came to be enriched by even more splendid and glowing colours, enhanced by the increased intensity of the light he used. At the same time, his treatment of historical subjects, borrowed from the usual repertory, altered in that the composition became simplified, the number of characters was reduced and he showed a preference for a form of dialogue restricted to two characters – unless, as often happened, he chose to portray the protagonist as a solitary figure, in which case the dialogue became a kind of confrontation with himself and represented his awareness of a destiny, felt through the eternal reality of one particular moment in time. Rembrandt must have been referring to the paintings belonging to this period when he said that his works had to be studied, and enjoyed, in a full light: therefore, as De Piles said (1715 edn.), 'although Rembrandt has treated subjects as they appear in all kinds of lights, it seems nevertheless that he endeavoured to place his models under a high and "enclosed" light . . . so that, the shadows being more intense and the illuminated parts more compact, objects appeared more true to life and more "sensitive"'' (*pls 52-68*).

In the last ten years of Rembrandt's life, the public became more and more impatient of his methods, but he still had a few official commissions. These he carried out without making any concessions to the wishes of his clients and with his usual total involvement in his personal vision. But the ideal of classical measure in art, which came about as the result of economic recession and its social repercussions, began to have adverse consequences for him, and led particularly to the disastrous reception, in 1662, of *The Conspiracy of Julius Civilis*. For, in my view, the rejection of this painting was due to the public's incomprehension of a view of the universe which remained firmly anchored in a rigorous realism, at a time when a serious crisis in art was affecting the whole of Dutch seventeenth-century culture. Rembrandt was the first victim of this crisis, which is hardly surprising in view of his radical participation in the preceding historical situation.

Yet, as we have seen, Rembrandt never allowed adversity to interrupt his work, however serious his financial difficulties, however great his grief for the death of those dear to him, however cruel the indifference of the public: in the private world of his studio, he patiently and methodically continued to seek inspiration in the inexhaustible world around him and to give form to the visions of his imagination (*pls 69-79*). As Hauser has written, only in the Dutch seventeenth century could Rembrandt have achieved the success that was temporarily his; but, conversely, in no other age or place would he have been so pitilessly and completely cast down. 'A courtly and conservative culture might perhaps not have made it possible for an artist of his stamp to make his mark; but once he had done so, it would perhaps have allowed him to maintain his position better than he was able to do in the middle-class, liberal society of Holland, which enabled him to develop freely, but crushed him as soon as he showed himself to be firm in his purpose.' We are moved and at the same time disquieted by Rembrandt's detachment from all the external events which touched his life, by his serene and profound love for life in its entirety and by his unflagging determination to express it as fully and completely as he possibly could.

Van Gogh once said that one cannot look at a Rembrandt without believing in God: this was, of course, an emotional reaction to what was probably a subconscious desire to receive the intimate communication of a religious experience which represented neither metaphysical nostalgia nor a surrender to mysticism, but the deeply felt experience of life in its human and earthly substance. This experience, representing a moment of 'consciousness' which was part of a very definite period of history, has been transmuted by Rembrandt into a form which has eternal validity.

# Rembrandt and the Critics

Much has been written about Rembrandt, and although he has aroused more interest at some periods than at others, he has never been totally ignored. Even during his lifetime, and while he was still a young man, he attracted the attention of his contemporaries, who were quick to recognize his gifts. As early as 1628, the Utrecht lawyer Aernout van Buchell, who was in Leyden in May of that year, referred to him in a note which was to have been incorporated in *Res Pictoriae*, a work which was never completed. Van Buchell wrote: 'The Leyden miller's son is greatly praised, but before his time.' This brief judgment established, in a quite extraordinary way, the line to be adopted later by biographers belonging to the realist school of criticism. Constantijn Huygens, in his *Autobiography* (which he began to write between 1629 and 1631), also mentions Rembrandt – and at greater length. His account is a description of the way in which Rembrandt and his partner Lievens worked, rather than a considered analysis of their art (edited by J. A. Worp, 1891).

The first biographical study of Rembrandt appeared in the second edition (Leyden, 1641) of *Beschrijvinge der Stadt Leyden* by J. Orlers, published when Rembrandt's fame already extended beyond the Netherlands and his works were becoming highly prized throughout Europe. In addition to this, Rembrandt's name began to appear more and more frequently in the 1650s and 1660s in the works of Dutch poets, who held a particularly esteemed and influential position in society: he was praised in the verses of Jan Zoet (1648), Lambert van den Bos (1650), Jeremias de Decker (1660), Jan Vos (1661-2), and even the great Joost van den Vondel accorded him respect and admiration. (For these mentions, see Seymour Slive, 1953.)

Internationally, critical interest and appreciation accompanied, or followed closely behind, the artist's commercial success. To give a few examples: the Flemish historian Cornelius de Bie writes of Rembrandt with great admiration in his *Het Gulden Cabinet* (1661); Guercino, in a letter dated 13 June 1660, told the Sicilian collector Don Antonio Ruffo that he regarded Rembrandt as 'a great virtuoso,' and that his engravings, several of which he had seen, 'are very successful, engraved in good taste and well made, from which one can deduce that his use of colour must be just as exquisite'; John Evelyn, in *Sculptura, or the History and Art of Chalcography* (1662), spoke of the 'incomparable Reinbrand' and the 'particular spirit' of his engravings; and Michel de Marolles, in the *Catalogue de Livre d'Estampes* (1672), refer to Rembrandt as one of the great etchers of all time.

The movement towards classicism, which occurred around the last quarter of the century, brought some reservations into the attitude of critics of Rembrandt's art. Some critics blamed him for ignoring *le bon goût* and neglecting to acquire the discipline which a study of classical antiquity would have given him. Among these were Joachim von Sandrart, in *L'Academia Tedesca dell'Architectura, Scultura et Pictura* (1675), Samuel van Hoogstraten (even though he was a pupil of Rembrandt), in *Inleyding tot de Hooge Schoole der Schilder-Konst anders de Zichtbaere Werelt* (1678), and Filippo Baldinucci, in *Cominciamento e progresso dell'arte dell'intagliamento in rame, colle vite di molti de' più eccellenti Maestri della stessa Professione* (1686): all these works contain useful biographical information and valuable descriptions of the artist's technique, made either from direct observation or from well-informed sources.

Critical opinion, however, was never entirely unfavourable: for example, the poet Andries Pels, after pointing out in his *Gebruick en misbruick des tooneels* (1681) that Rembrandt had failed in *imitatio naturae* (a classical concept) and deprecating his indiscriminate copying of the vulgar aspects of nature, finally admitted that he had nevertheless created his own, aesthetically justified nature. The same is true of the criticism of the more vehement classicists who followed Sandrart. André Félibien, with his *Entretiens sur les vies et sur les ouvrages de plus excellents peintres* (1685), belongs to this class and, more especially, admirers of the school of Poussin, whose influence was apparent in the

*Abrégé de la vie des peintres, avec des réflexions sur leurs ouvrages* by Roger de Piles (1699). According to De Piles, it is useless to look in Rembrandt's work for 'either correctness of draughtsmanship or taste for the antique'; he admits, however, that these qualities are not relevant to Rembrandt's art, because his personal genius enabled him to arrive at workable and up-to-date conclusions while ignoring all preconceived ideas or theories.

The ideas propounded by De Piles proved extremely fertile during the following decades: for example, in the epigrams published by John Elsum in *Epigrams upon the Paintings of the Most Eminent Masters, Ancient and Modern* (1700); and in the French translation of the Richardsons' critical studies, published in 1728 under the title *Description de divers fameux tableaux*, where emphasis is laid on the value of 'expressiveness' in Rembrandt's art. Following this example, Antoine Coypel, in his *Discours prononcé dans les Conférences de l'Académie Royale de Peinture et de Sculpture* (1721), states that Rembrandt's art has the merit at least of considerable technical skill, which leaves nothing to chance and may be compared with that of the great Italian masters of the Renaissance, or with that of Poussin, although the aims of these artists were different from his.

Arnold Houbraken's biography of Rembrandt, which appeared in the first volume of *Groote Schounbourgh de Nederlantsche en Schilderessen* (1718), contains criticism following these traditional lines, and tries to show Rembrandt's unique position in Dutch seventeenth-century art (as Gérard de Lairesse had done in his *Groot Schilderboeck*, 1714). It also provides a useful historical record, in that Houbraken draws up a catalogue of the paintings and gives some new information concerning Rembrandt's life and artistic career. This work of criticism later became, for better or worse, the point of reference for the critical studies on Rembrandt produced during the eighteenth century and, to a certain extent, for those of the nineteenth century as well. At the same time, parallel with this type of criticism, there grew up a critical attitude which saw in Rembrandt a master of the *manière noire*, beginning with the poetry of Joos van den Vondel and brought out more explicitly in Florent Le Comte's *Cabinet des singularités d'architecture, peinture, sculpture et gravure* (1699). This attitude was to have a considerable following, especially during the romantic period.

To turn to a new chapter in the history of criticism, Taillasson, in *Observations sur quelques peintres* (1807), rejected the reservations made by the classicist and academic school of criticism, and declared that, on the contrary, if Rembrandt had observed the rules which those writers regarded as sacrosanct, or had paid the usual tribute of the *voyage d'Italie*, this would probably have resulted in a prettifying of his art, to the detriment of the creation of 'a new race of magicians, who interest all men, just as tales of sorcerers interest all children.' In fact, Sir Joshua Reynolds, in *Journey to Flanders and Holland in the Year 1781* (in *The Literary Works of Sir Joshua Reynolds*, collected by H. W. Beechy, 1850), had already expressed his unqualified admiration for Rembrandt, which was to be echoed by all the great painters of the following century, from Delacroix (in his *Journal* and *Letters*) to Van Gogh (*Letters*).

The first decidedly 'modern' interpretation of Rembrandt – after the important catalogue of the engravings drawn up by A. Bartsch (*Catalogue raisonné de toutes les estampes*, 1797) – is to be found in C. Josi's *Imitation de dessins d'aprés les maîtres hollandais et flamands* (1821). Josi counteracted the arguments of the academicians and purists, and indicated a new approach to Rembrandt's work: 'This rare genius all at once transcended the narrow bounds set for him by the rules and his mentors.' His partiality was, of course, as marked as that of his opponents, and his enthusiasm was later echoed by Théophile Gautier in *Esquisse de voyage* (1845-6), and by other impenitent adherents to this point of view, such as the Flemish poet E. Verhaeren.

However, with the advent of modern criticism, it has become more and more common for historians to seek an objective and impartial view of Rembrandt's art, a view based on the facts alone. Moreover, as we approach modern times, the body of writing on Rembrandt becomes so vast that it is impossible to list more than the most important works. These are as follows:

Eugène Fromentin, *Maîtres d'autrefois*, Paris 1877; C. Hofstede de Groot, ed., *Die Urkunden über Rembrandt, 1575-1721*, The Hague 1906, an indispensable guide for any documentary study; Wilhelm R. Valentiner, *Rembrandt, Des Meisters Gemälde*, Stuttgart 1908; G. Simmel, *Rembrandt, ein Kunstphilosophischer Versuch*, 1919; A. M. Hind, *Rembrandt's Etchings*, 2 vols, London 1923; Otto Benesch, *Rembrandt, Werk und Forschung*, 1935, for an excellent bibliography; H. Focillon, *Rembrandt*, 1935; A. Bredius, *The Paintings of Rembrandt*, complete edition, London 1937; Johan Huizinga, *Nederland's Beschaving in de Zeventiende Eeuw*, 1941, for historial background; Jacob Rosenberg, *Rembrandt*, 2 vols, 1948; L. Münz, *The Etchings of Rembrandt*, 2 vols, 1952; Seymour Slive, *Rembrandt and his Critics, 1630-1730*, The Hague 1953; Otto Benesch, *Rembrandt's Drawings*, 6 vols, London 1954-7; Catalogue of the exhibition of paintings, etchings and drawings held at the Rijksmuseum, Amsterdam, 1956; L. Goldscheider, *Rembrandt: Paintings, Drawings and Etchings*, Cambridge, Mass., 1960; Kenneth Clark, *Rembrandt and the Italian Renaissance*, London 1966; Kurt Bauch, *Rembrandt Gemälde*, Berlin 1966.

# Notes on the Plates

**1 Samson and Delilah, 1628.** Oil on panel, 59.5×49.5 cm. Berlin, Gemäldegalerie Berlin-Dahlem. Signed and dated: RL 1628. Based on *Judges* 16: 19-20.

**2 St Anastasius, 1631.** Oil on panel, 60×48 cm. Stockholm, National Museum. Signed and dated: REMBRANT FC 1631.

**3-6 The Anatomy lesson of Professor Tulp, 1632.** Oil on canvas, 162.5×216.5 cm. The Hague, Mauritshuis. Signed and dated: REMBRANDT F 1632. This painting represents the anatomy lesson given by Dr Nicolaes Tulp on 31 January 1632, when he dissected the body of a certain Adrian Adriansz, an arrow-maker of Leyden, who had been hanged for criminal offences the previous day.

**7 Self-portrait, c. 1633.** Oil on panel, 62×52 cm. Florence, Uffizi. The lower section of this painting has been cut, and perhaps also (according to Bredius, 1937) something off each side.

**8 Self-portrait with Saskia, c. 1635.** Oil on canvas, 161×131 cm. Dresden, Gemäldegalerie. Signed: REMBRANDT F.

**9 The Descent from the Cross, 1633.** Oil on canvas, 93×68 cm. Munich, Alte Pinakothek. Signed: REMBRANT F. Painted for Stadtholder Frederick Henry.

**10-11 Artemisia, 1634.** Oil on canvas, 142×135 cm. Madrid, Prado. Signed and dated: REMBRANDT F 1634. The subject has sometimes been thought to be Sophonisba (Bredius, 1937), after Livy xxx, 15.

**12 The Rape of Ganymede, 1635.** Oil on canvas, 171×130 cm. Dresden, Gemäldegalerie. Signed and dated: REMBRANDT FT 1635.

**13-15 Danaë, 1636.** Oil on canvas, 185×203 cm. Leningrad, Hermitage. Signed and dated: REMBRANDT F 1636.

**16 Elazar Swarmius, 1637.** Oil on canvas, 139×109 cm. Antwerp, Musée Royal des Beaux-Arts. Signed and dated: REMBRANDT F 1637.

**17 Self-portrait, 1637.** Oil on panel, 80×62 cm. Paris, Louvre. Signed and dated: REMBRANDT F 1637.

**18-19 Samson's wedding, 1638.** Oil on canvas, 126.5×175.5 cm. Dresden, Gemäldegalerie. Signed and dated: REMBRANDT F 1638.

**20  Rembrandt's mother, 1639.** Oil on panel, 79.5×61.7 cm. Vienna, Kunsthistorisches Museum. Signed and dated: REMBRANDT F 1639.

**21  The Entombment of Christ, 1639.** Oil on canvas, 93×69 cm. Munich, Alte Pinakothek. The date of this painting is known from a letter written by Rembrandt to Constantijn Huygens (C. Hofstede de Groot, 1906).

**22  Landscape with castle, c. 1640.** Oil on panel, 44.5×90 cm. Paris, Louvre. Most historians agree in dating this work about 1640.

**23-4  The Visitation, 1640.** Oil on panel, 56.5×49 cm. Detroit, Institute of Arts. Signed and dated: REMBRANDT 1640.

**25-32  Parade of the Civic Guard under Captain F. Banning Cocq (The Night Watch), 1642.** Oil on canvas, 359×438 cm. Amsterdam, Rijcksmuseum. Signed and dated: REMBRANDT F 1642.

**33  David taking leave of Jonathan, 1642.** Oil on panel, 73×61.5 cm. Leningrad, Hermitage. Signed and dated: REMBRANDT F 1642.

**34-6  The Woman taken in adultery, 1644.** Oil on panel, 83.8×65.4 cm. London, National Gallery. Signed and dated: REMBRANDT F 1644.

**37-8  The Holy Family with angels, 1645.** Oil on canvas, 117×91 cm. Leningrad, Hermitage. Signed and dated: REMBRANDT F 1645.

**39  Young girl leaning on the lower part of a door, 1645.** Oil on canvas, 100×84 cm. The Art Institute of Chicago. Signed and dated: REMBRANDT F 1645.

**40-1  Susanna and the two elders, 1647.** Oil on panel, 76×91 cm. Berlin, Gemäldegalerie. Signed and dated: REMBRANDT F 1647.

**42  Christ at Emmaus, 1648.** Oil on panel, 65×68 cm. Paris, Louvre. Signed and dated: REMBRANDT F 1648.

**43  Portrait of a Jew, c. 1648.** Oil on panel, 24.5×20.5 cm. Berlin, Gemäldegalerie. An oil sketch.

**44-5  Self-portrait, 1650.** Oil on canvas, 91.7×73.6 cm. Washington, National Gallery (Widener Coll.) Signed and dated: REMBRANDT F 1650.

**46-7  Large equestrian portrait, 1649 or 1663.** Oil on canvas, 295×241 cm. London, National Gallery. Signed and dated: REMBRANDT F (followed by an indecipherable date).

**48  Man with a gilt helmet, c. 1652.** Oil on canvas, 67.5×51.5 cm. Berlin, Gemäldegalerie.

**49-50  The Vision of Daniel, after 1650.** Oil on canvas, 96×116 cm. Berlin, Gemäldegalerie.

**51  Old man with red cap, c. 1653.** Oil on canvas, 51×37 cm. Berlin, Gemäldegalerie.

**52  Slaughtered ox, 1655.** Oil on canvas, 94×67 cm. Paris, Louvre. Signed and dated: REMBRANDT F 1655.

**53  Self-portrait, 1652.** Oil on canvas, 50×41 cm. Vienna, Kunsthistorisches Museum.

**54-5  Self-portrait, c. 1659.** Oil on canvas, 85×69.5 cm. London, National Gallery.

**56  A woman bathing in a stream (Hendrickje Stoffels?), 1655.** Oil -on canvas, 62×47 cm. London, National Gallery. Signed and dated: REMBRANDT F 1655. Bredius (1937) believed this to be a portrait of Hendrickje.

**57  Bathsheba at her toilet, 1654.** Oil on canvas, 142×142 cm. Paris, Louvre. Signed and dated: REMBRANDT F 1654.

**58-60  Potiphar's wife accusing Joseph, 1655.** Oil on canvas, 105×97 cm. Washington, National Gallery (Mellon Coll.). Signed and dated: REMBRANDT F 1655. Formerly in the Hermitage, Leningrad.

**61  Christ and the woman of Samaria, 1655.** Oil on panel, 46.5×39 cm. Berlin, Gemäldegalerie. Signed and dated: REMBRANDT F 1655.

**62  David harping before Saul, c. 1658.** Oil on canvas, 130.5×164 cm. The Hague, Mauritshuis.

**63  Titus reading, before 1659.** Oil on canvas, 70.5×64 cm. Vienna, Kunsthistorisches Museum.

**64  Old man, c. 1658-9.** Oil on canvas, 102×83 cm. Florence, Uffizi. Signed: REMBRANDT F 16?? (only the first two figures of the date are legible).

**65-6  The Descent from the Cross, c. 1658.** Oil on canvas, 143.5×106.6 cm. Washington, National Gallery (Widener Coll.). Signed: REMBRANDT F 165? (only the first three figures of the date are legible).

**67-8  Philemon and Baucis, 1658.** Oil on panel, 54.6×68.6 cm. Washington, National Gallery (Widener Coll.). Signed and dated: REMBRANDT F 1658.

**69  Moses, 1659.** Oil on canvas, 167×135 cm. Berlin, Gemälde-galerie. Signed and dated: REMBRANDT F 1659.

**70  Self-portrait, 1659.** Oil on canvas, 68×53 cm. Washington, National Gallery (Mellon Coll.). Signed and dated: REMBRANDT F 1659.

**71-3  The Apostle Paul, c. 1660.** Oil on canvas, 129×102 cm. Washington, National Gallery (Widener Coll.). Signed: REMBRANDT F.

**74  The Evangelist Matthew, 1661.** Oil on panel, 23×19 cm. Washington, National Gallery. Signed and dated: REMBRANDT F 1661.

**75  Two Negroes, 1661.** Oil on canvas, 77.8×64.4 cm. The Hague, Mauritshuis. Signed and dated: REMBRANDT F 1661.

**The Conspiracy of Julius Civilis, 1662.** Monochrome illustration on p. 9. Oil on canvas, 196×309 cm. Stockholm, Academy. The subject of this work was taken from the *Histories* of Tacitus (IV, 13-16). It was commissioned for Amsterdam's town hall, rebuilt after the disastrous fire of 1552, but was rejected. It was intended that the subject, the revolt of the Batavians led by Julius Civilis against the Romans, should symbolize the spirit of the Dutch nation. The painting has come down to us in a damaged condition (the original measurements must have been about 550×550 cm.): but it is possible to reconstruct the whole composition from the preparatory sketch made by Rembrandt, which is now in the Kupferstichkabinett, Munich.

**76  Self-portrait, c. 1661-2.** Oil on canvas, 70×55.5 cm. Florence, Uffizi.

**77  The Presentation in the Temple, c. 1662.** Oil on canvas, 98.5×79.5 cm. Stockholm, National Museum. A late work, probably unfinished.

**78-9  The Return of the Prodigal Son, c. 1665.** Oil on canvas, 265×205 cm. Leningrad, Hermitage. This painting carries a signature which has been proved false.

1

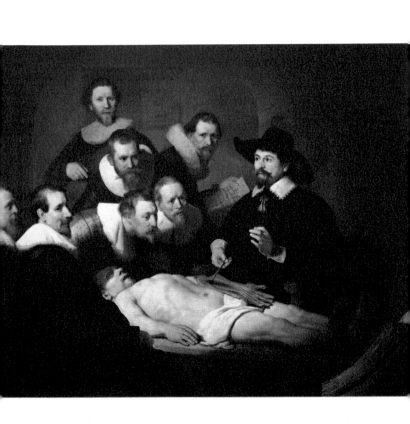

9

Rembrandt 1640

40

41

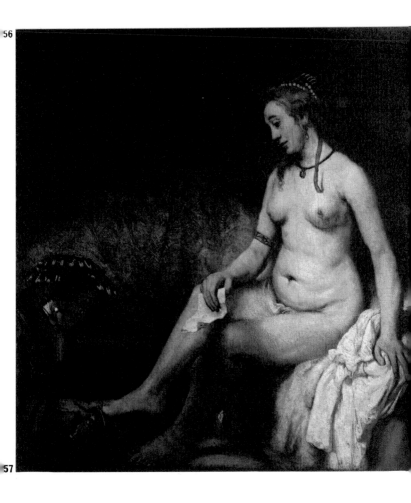

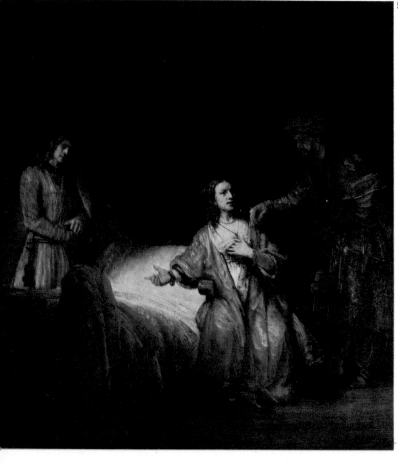

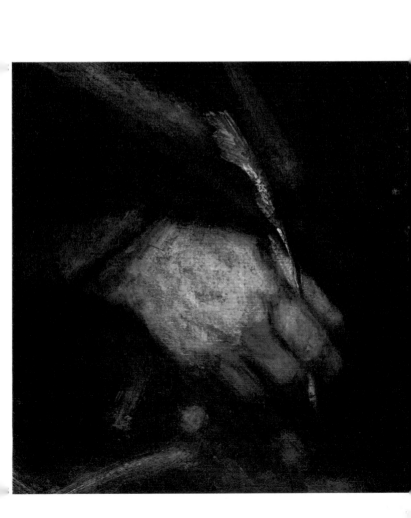